"This Is Not a Place To Sing"

Poems by Christina Pacosz

West End Press

ISBN 0-931122-47-3

West End Press • P.O. Box 27334 • Albuquerque, NM 87125

TABLE OF CONTENTS

To those of larger sight
the rim of shadow
is a line
of light.

*From an abandoned Detroit theatre
marquee 8/6/85*

On the Possibility of Poetics as Revolution

for Fredy Perlman, 1935–1985

When I write
words on paper
I am a dog
howling

listening
to the engines
and ambulances
rushing to disaster
and destruction.

I can only
mark
their passage.

With profound gratitude to the anonymous
Polish woman in the Auschwitz Museum's
coffee shop, who gently admonished a
group of Polish youth singing in their
enthusiasm at a holiday outing, "This
is not a place to sing," for the title of
this collection.

Also thanks to the Kosciuszko Foundation
for the opportunity to study and travel
in Poland.

I.
Droga Polska*

*Dear Poland

The Wind at the Wedding

The wind lifts the hem of the bride's dress. She is wearing white shoes. Her feet look frail surrounded by the hard stones of the street, the raised hoop of her skirt. The bride is a bell for a moment, waiting to be rung.

Unlike the wind, who is a traveler, the bride is stationary and may never leave Lublin. Possibly she will visit the Black Sea on a holiday with her husband, but she will not be wearing her white dress. She will never be a bell again, all the notes wrung out of her, whether she remains in a flat in Lublin, or suns herself on the sand.

The wind is an old wind, full of understanding, but, like the bride's feet, it has no strength against the stones of the street. No strength to lift the people's hearts, even for a moment. The wind has only enough strength to lift the white hem of the dress of the bride who is wearing white shoes with high heels to match her high hopes.

The groom has white gloves on his hands. The stones at his feet are grey. The stones are grey and as old as the wind, maybe older.

In Krakow, there are fossils embedded in the paving stones around St. Mary's Church. There, the brides and grooms step on ancient animals without thinking. There, when the trumpeter plays his notes from the steeple, he imagines he is flinging his song to the sky, which is like the sea, blue and roiled, but by swallows, not fish. What does it matter: fish, fowl, human flesh? We all share the same fate.

The bride and groom are waiting for the bells to ring, for permission to become one flesh. The wind lifts her dress and the bride does not blush when the groom stares at her feet. Why should she?

The wind blowing its way through the old city is a kind wind. Wise and kind and old like a grandfather or grandmother. The bride and groom may be thinking that one day *this* day will lead them to a garden and grandchildren climbing on their laps in the sun. Peace.

The bride and groom are young. They have never known war, but the wind cannot forget how it blows over the eyelids of the dead in all directions. Today the wind wants to play a simple joke and lift a bride's dress, showing her shoes, her ankles to the world.

The wind harbors no illusions. To lift a dress is not to lift a heart, except maybe his, the groom's, who is staring at the bride's ankles, thinking how they will be his soon. He wants to kiss the blue vein under the strap of her shoe. He wants to begin there.

The wind knows the hearts of the people are hungry, but for what? Meat lines, milk lines, bread lines, lines for vodka. Lines on the palms of his hands, the map of his life lost to a grenade in the Warsaw Uprising.

What is the soldier doing here? Isn't this a wedding, not a war?

In this country there is too much to remember. Better to watch the wind lift the hem of the bride's white dress like a cloud moving across the grey stones into the church.

Baba Yaga Speculates

> Thou liftest me up on the wind,
> thou makest me ride on it,
> and thou tossest me about
> in the roar of the storm.
>
> *Job 30:22*

What if I had lived
a life of prayer
on my knees
in the dark, at dawn?
Prayer in the fields,
beneath the feather quilt.
Marking the loaf
before it is sliced.

Thunder, hail, lightning
beating an indifferent sky
and on earth nothing
to challenge the wind,
the land hunched
even in the best
of weather.

Walls of water and wind
and mud at my feet, my knees
weakened by incense
and dim light.

If I open
my mouth
I could
drown.

At Morskie Oko Lake, Zakopane

It is a grey country
even when the sky is blue
and today it is raining.

Mist gathers itself,
a quiet fist
clutching the mountains.

Nuns in grey habits
walk over grey rocks
circling the lake.

If this is too much grey,
look at the trees, green
bodies, beds of moss

waiting, the small blue
eyes of *niezapominajki**
watching.

The nuns have disappeared
and only the shore of the lake,
the eye of the sea,

is visible, a narrow
border of aquamarine
filled with trout flicking

tails in the cold water,
swimming in the only
sky there is.

*forget-me-nots

The Trumpeter of Krakow

I swear on my honor as a Pole,
as a servant of the King of the Polish
people, that I will faithfully and
unto the death, if there be need, sound
upon the trumpet the Heynal in honor
of Our Lady each hour in the Tower of
the church which bears Her Name.

Ancient oath of the Trumpeter of Krakow

The whole city listens
when the trumpeter plays.
People open their ears
and look up at the sky,
cloudy today or a hazy
blue, smeared with dirt
from Nowa Huta's steel
mills. A whole country
of ears waiting
for the broken note,
as if listening
could make the song
complete.

I am listening, too,
and the listening does
heal the brokenness
like the flash of color
on a butterfly's wing
makes us happy
when we are not.

The trumpeter plays the hour
and has for 800 years
since the Tartars
surrounded him, reminding
all who listen:

Each of us
is invaded
daily, hourly,
minute by minute
by time
and its deadly
arrows.

How to sing
from the highest steeple
and warn the city
with the sounds
that live
in us
and the world?

Matka Boska, Matka Polska*

1.

All the women here are mothers with capable hands and patient
feet. Hands that wash and sew, chop vegetables and slice meat.
Feet that wait in line for trams, buses, taxis. Meat, milk, bread.
An entire country criss-crossed with lines where women wait,
standing on tired feet for whatever they need to buy.

Feet splayed like river deltas. Gnarled like oak roots. Legs
swollen, blue veins popping. Looking at these feet you'd think
the entire population of women aged. But no, gaze at the faces,
they are young, younger than the feet.

"They also serve who stand and wait." This is not a Party
slogan, but could be, red and black shouting from white
banners slung across boulevards and buildings. The priests
teach, serve God and man. The women learn their lesson well.

2.

I dream I am in the museum at Czestochowa where Walesa's
portrait hangs with those of kings, surrounded by golden
objects, amber statuary, jeweled swords and mother-of-pearl
rosaries. Lech's Nobel medal is under glass, alongside other
notable mementoes.

I dream there is a poster of white cardboard printed with black
letters and tacked to a free space on the wall. This is for
Danuta, his wife. This is something, but enough?

*Mother of God, Mother of Poland

The Shrine of the Black Madonna at Czestochowa

> You are the light of the world,
> A city set on a hill
> cannot be hid.
>
> *Matthew 5:14*

A multitude, such as Jesus must have spoken to, swells the cathedral. What century is this? You are the destination of a blood-red tunnel. The old mother, icon of a people. I am gazing into a birth canal, being pushed toward you, and you are the world I am entering.

A world that is in the world, but not of it, where my heart is a spring of clear water, cold and fresh. A world where joy sits on my lap always. A world where pain is seasonal and you birth all of it. Again and again taking illness and death into you to make the new moon of beginnings possible.

The people surrounding me are ripples breaking on the rim of a pool deep in the mountains. *And they hold me up.*

There is an old woman behind me who cannot see you, she is so stooped. I turn to one side, my eyes riveted on you. We rise and kneel again. The woman cannot. I offer her my arm and she pulls herself up. And down again, leaning on me. I am weeping. We are both smiling. While you watch.

Rafting the Dunajec

We step into the boat
and the gypsies are playing
accordians one-handed,
the other extended palm up.

I am so glad
they are alive
I give them money
for that reason.

The river claims
the boat and I give
myself to the water
and the skill
of the raftsmen,
caps strung
with cowrie shells,
plastic now, but once,
the real item from
the Black Sea.

There are willow
and birch on shore
and storks *cra-aanking*
in nests.

We come to the gorge
and the wind off the high peaks
washes us with the odor
of spruce, rosemary, pepper.

I say to myself: If
I knew a song
I would sing
and then I hear
a raft of children

singing across the water,
and I am happy,
just like I am happy
when I hear
the water
as it meets
the rocks.

St. Stanislaus Church, Warsaw,
Father Jerzy Popieluszko's Grave

Though we are far
from the sea, here
is an anchor resting
in the sun, beached
on the grass.

I offer purple
and red gladioli,
a few among thousands
of blooms.

When I kneel
I remember
"Give us this day
our daily bread,"
but this is not
how I pray.

If we are anchored
in sorrow the storm
will suck us under
where the rocks wait.

We must cut loose
and sail, without
instruments,

just the heavenly bodies
and our own sense
of direction,

to other
more hospitable
shores.

In the Country

Here the patchwork quilt
of earth is visible
from the ground, no need
for an aerial view.

The planted fields
are tablecloths spread
over the land:

a swatch of brown here,
gold there and green
of all descriptions.

A cow or two staked out,
a few sheep tethered.
No fences.

The storks like that.
They can walk where
they will, clacking beaks
at each other, reminiscing
about Egypt.

Humans labor
at these tables
by hand and foot,
with hoes and scythes
and patient horses.

No mono-crops
stretching the horizon
but a landscape
of human proportions,
made for the bent back
and the long haul.

A Sunday Walk On Kosciuszko Mountain, Krakow*

They build mountains here
by hand, clod by clod,
shovel to barrow,
until a hill
crafted by humans
rises green
and forested.

A body stretched
across the horizon
sleeping under
the blue quilt
of sky.

*A hill created a few years after Thaddeus Kosciuszko's death
in 1817 with soil from Polish and American battlefields, where
he was a commander of American troops during the
Revolutionary War

Some Thoughts on the Polish Custom of Greeting Every Occasion With Flowers

That last night
in the ancient capital
there are flowers
at my feet
as I step
onto the tram.

Lupine and pansy
in a nosegay,
purple against
the dense black
of the street.

I pick the bouquet
crushing the flowers
to my face
where the tears
are waiting.

II.

How to Put a Name to This

. . . It was the organizational skill
of the Nazis rather than their new
weapons that made the society of
total domination a reality . . .

. . . The Germans demonstrated that a
modern state can successfully organize
an entire people for its own extermination . . .

. . . Of supreme importance as a weapon
of bureaucratic domination is the
modern computer. Few weapons were
as indispensable to the Gestapo as
its files . . .

The Cunning of History, The Holocaust and the American Future
Richard L. Rubenstein

The Jewish Cemetery, Warsaw

> By the waters of Babylon,
> there we sat down and wept,
> when we remembered Zion.
> On the willows there
> we hung up our lyres.
> For there our captors
> required of us songs,
> and our tormentors, mirth, saying,
> "Sing us one of the songs of Zion!"
>
> *Psalm 137*

Only the trees sing now,
rustling above us.
Poplar, oak and mountain ash
conversing in
a universal language
rooted in the soil.

Few visit the dead
and those who do
often weep.
Some come with malice still
and there are recent swastikas
scratched on marble —

> *What weapon was used?*
> *A nail, a pick, a spike,*
> *Christ on the cross.*

There is a newly reconstructed
wall around this Jerusalem,
forgotten by the new people
of a new city, a modern phoenix
stretching its wings
by the Vistula.

One inhabitant remembers:

A Pole, a Christian, old enough
to have done what? during the war.
He dresses in traditional Jewish garb,
a solitary crow perched
at the door
of the only
synagogue remaining.

He does not dare enter,
but mutters to himself,
"Lord, I am not worthy,
not worthy."

He comes to this cemetery
laden with pine boughs,
carrying brightly painted
wooden plaques honoring
the twentieth anniversary
of the death
of Bernard Mark, a Jewish
scholar. *And what
prayer does he recite?*

>Your eyes are
>upon me

>I cannot
>forget

Auschwitz: Oswiecim

Los Nas Dla Was Przestroga
(Let Our Loss Be Your Warning)

Majdanek Monument

We are leaving
flowers like messages
in this awful place:

what else to do
except fall down
with weeping
into a grieving
that will never
be done.

And how to live
in the world then?

So it is calendula
for memory, here
with the children's
clothing they never
outgrew.

And here before
hundreds of neatly
lettered suitcases
with addresses from
every country in Europe
never claimed
by their owners
we leave
our innocence
in the form
of a single
white daisy.

We should haul
larkspur by
the truckload

and fill every
exhibit room
from floor to ceiling
with levity
with light.

We must airdrop
hyacinth, purple
sorrow raining down
until this place
of the awful name
is smothered in
fragrance.

We should be weaving
miles of rosemary garlands
for remembrance
and planting olive
for peace.

The lilac leaves
are waving, try
to imagine
them blooming.

The poplar trees
are voices
in the wind:

> We did not
> consent
> that our bodies
> be used
> as weapons.
>
> Remember the ash
> how it sifts down
> to the desks
> where the bureaucrats
> are stamping papers.

For the Man With Swastikas in His Eyes

"I was in Japan
mopping up
after Hiroshima
and Nagasaki
when I got the news
about the death camps.

I was horrified
human beings
could do such
awful things.

No, it's not
the same.
Those bombs
saved my butt.

Not the same
at all."

A Message From the Past For the Present

A looming mound
of empty zyklon B canisters
behind glass: to open death
like canned peaches.

Behind the tins:
corporate profit.

Are there no new tales
we can tell each other?

Artifacts of the age,
the waning twentieth century
on parade, naked
and exhausted.

Each time capsule
should include
one of these.

Such eloquent
refuse.

On the Propensity of the Human Species to Repeat Error

> And if they kill others for being who they are
> or where they are
> Is this a law of history
> or simply, *what must change?*
>
> *Your Native Land, Your Life*
> Adrienne Rich

The world is round.
This should tell us
something, this should
have been our first clue.

> *what goes around*
> *comes around*

Scientists are studying
a rent in the roof of sky
over the South Pole
right now, but poets
need not adhere
to the caution
of the scientific method.

The message is simple:

> *what goes around*
> *comes around*

The battery acid of
Plato's Republic
has finally reached
the ozone layer,
a membrane, protective
like skin or an amniotic sac,

permeable and destructible.

what we take
for granted
will get us
in the end

The Sioux woman's breast
severed from her body,
dried into a pouch
for tobacco,
what book was that?

Or a chosen people's skin
stretched across the heavens,
shade for us to more easily
read the harsh lesson
of history.

Krakow Monument to the Martyred

What is it like
to have your heart
torn out and live?

Some know the answer
to this painful question,
but most are dead.

This monolith is erected
to their memory
by a familiar tribe:
twentieth century man.

And we are archaeologists
come to witness
the monumental failure
of the human heart.

A jagged slash of lightning
rips through the breasts
of the five figures
and there is an opening
in the stone.

A space through which
light travels
and we can see
a cloudy sky.

Krakow Monument: Another View

There are always those
who would kill
the singer.
Remember
we describe the voice
as "dying away."

We often speak
of the natural world
like that, a metaphor
we say for an ending,
though we are convinced
only humans suffer death,
and then some more
than others.

Outside Krakow the *ogrodki**
hum with summer.
They sing! we say, and think
the simple declarative enough.

Another of history's lies,
these old, tired tales
we keep repeating, as if
there is nothing new
under the sun,

but there is.

The sky is falling,
while the sun shines
and the fields grow
their hair, lush
from the ash.

*Garden plots cultivated by city residents

We are burning,
the iron rumble
of the ovens
dry thunder

invading our sleep.

On the Nature of All Memorials

Too little.
Too late.

For Dr. Janusz Korczak* Who Was
Not Afraid to Sing

At the end
of the line
he knew
what
to do.

Walking
from the boxcar
to the gas chamber
he led the children

singing.

*Director of the Jewish orphanage in Warsaw during the Nazi
occupation

III.

Moja Droga Rodzina*

*My Dear Family

Candles In the Storm

What a familiar gesture!
Small comfort
against the odds
that assail. I, too,
have lit my share
out of necessity,

that mother of invention.

What other weapons
can we bring to bear?

For *Ciotka**
Felinow, August, 1986

We are cutting
off the poppies' heads
long after
the bloom.

It is the seed
we want.

Add egg, sugar, flour
and vanilla:
poppyseed cake.

My mouth waters
as we walk
the row, gathering
dried stalks
into our arms.

I tell you I will keep
one pod. When
I shake it, thousands
of miles away, the quiet
sound the seeds make
will remind me of you,
the crone of the family.

Your head spins, your heart
hurts and all
the food you eat
comes back
to trouble you.

*aunt

You do not like
to think
of yourself
as dried up.

A dried-up woman
takes up room
by the fire.

So you stand and cook
all day, walking across
the muddy yard
to climb the wood pile
in search
of the driest pieces.

How is it
that wood
and poppyseeds
are at their best
when dried,

but you are not?

The Assumption of the Blessed Virgin Mary, August 15

1.

She has gone
to heaven
where she will
intercede
for us.

She is the earth
and cannot
forget us.

Last night
under a half moon
she rose
with the smoke
from the burning
stubble, a bonfire
in the fields
lighting her way.

When she passed
the moon
she cast
a shadow:

this dream:

Through the muddy
fields of Felinow
three women
come to me

to show me a spring.

I search for it
all day
in every leaf
and lark.

2.

My aunt arranges
a bouquet
her daughter-in-law
has gathered
to be blessed
in church.

Mach,* buckwheat, barley, millet,
dill, dahlias, asparagus fern,
cabbage leaf, daisies, gladioli,
green beans, roses and phlox.

And when the next cow calves,
the dried bloom
will sweeten her
first drinking water,
and Mary's blessing
flow from her udders.

3.

The sow and her ten piglets
roam the locked farmyard.
I sit on a stool
in the mud and sun.

We are all on holiday.

The odor of chamomile
strong as church incense
after the rain
and the pigs' rooting.

*poppyseed

42

The sow makes
a deep sound
in her foraging,
and the piglets run
on tiny hooves
through the mud

toward her.

4.

A woman wearing
a white head scarf
and a red dress
walks the rutted road
on her way
to church,

carrying a bouquet.

Two Women, a Piano, a Clock

In the city there is a piano
in a crowded room in a small flat.

Each time she plays the keys
she thinks of hours
at the school
drilling scales.

In the country there is a clock
that chimes in a small house.

Each time she climbs a chair
and winds the clock
she remembers the pigs
raised to buy it.

Homesick

The flash
of swallow's wing
out the window

and the geranium

the only brightness
in the day.

The Homeplace Visited

1.

The land has forgotten
him, only a child
when he left. The apple trees
he helped plant are ripe again,
another harvest in the sixty-some
since he's been gone.

The orchard does not remember
him, how tenderly
he packed dirt
around roots
and tamped soil
so carefully
around each slender trunk.

The trees remember only bud
and blossom, fruit
and harvest, then
the long sleep of winter.

Only she remembers him,
the eldest, and she says little,
her life long days of work,
work, work.

The apples fall and rot,
more work, to pick, to cook,
tending the fire half the day,
and then a short,
unsatisfying sleep.

2.

The sun strides across
the fields and the potatoes
flex white muscle
in the sodden ground.

3.

My father remembers another life,
one burned in the ovens,
buried in the earth.

Who mourns the Jews?
A forgotten people, foreigners
who did not worship Christ
but waited for him
until destruction
claimed them.

My father waits, too,
thinking maybe he should
have stayed
and died here
with them,
the shopkeepers
and red-headed women,
the children tending
goats and geese.